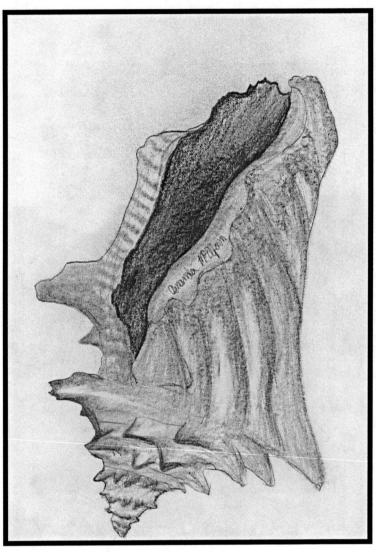

Conch Shell

KEY WEST'S

LITTLE GIRL OF OLDEN DAYS

Printed in Victoria, Canada

Note for Librarians: a cataloguing record for this book that includes Dewey Classification and US Library of Congress numbers is available from the National Library of Canada. The complete cataloguing record can be obtained from the National Library's online database at:
www.nlc-bnc.ca/amicus/index-e.html

ISBN 1-4120-1837-4

TRAFFORD

This book was published on-demand in cooperation with Trafford Publishing.
On-demand publishing is a unique process and service of making a book available for retail sale to the public taking advantage of on-demand manufacturing and Internet marketing. On-demand publishing includes promotions, retail sales, manufacturing, order fulfilment, accounting and collecting royalties on behalf of the author.

Suite 6E, 2333 Government St., Victoria, B.C. V8T 4P4, CANADA
Phone   250-383-6864   Toll-free 1-888-232-4444 (Canada & US)
Fax   250-383-6804   E-mail   sales@trafford.com
Web site www.trafford.com   TRAFFORD PUBLISHING IS A DIVISION OF TRAFFORD HOLDINGS LTD.
Trafford Catalogue #03-2214   www.trafford.com/robots/03-2214.html
10   9   8   7   6   5   4   3

Key West's Little Girl
Of
Olden Days

My Childhood

By
Florence Drudge Davis

Illustration and Back Cover
By
Amanda McElfresh

ACKNOWLEDGMENTS

As I put myself in a position of remembrance, I first want to acknowledge, to all my family, the overwhelming joys I have received over the years in being a part of their precious lives and I will cherish those experiences, which became unforgettable memories, for as long as the moon endures.

To my husband, Delmar, I am grateful for his belief in me and his patience and encouragement, while I dictated a new way of life for us both.

To my daughter, Nancy, I am deeply grateful for her interest in me and my project - always giving me words of encouragement. I also acknowledge her willingness to be interrupted just any old time, to share her expertise in referencing and cross-referencing biblical text from just random words, ideas, or meanings I could offer. Her guidance in spelling and correct word-usages came in handy and shortened my research time. I appreciate all of her efforts on my behalf.

I am appreciative of my son, Greg, a biblical scholar and writer, for his invaluable insights - recognizing some of the phraseology I used during our conversation was needed in my book and to use more of the same. I will always be grateful to him for his inspiration in promoting "my way with words."

To my daughter, Lorna, I would like to express my deepest gratitude for innumerable hours she devoted to me, for without her, this book would never have reached fruition. I will forever be grateful to her, first and foremost, for believing in me; giving me an "open-door" policy to her home and computer equipment, which included many sleepovers…anything it took to fit me in between her busy schedules, she graciously obliged.

I was thankful for her patience, over and beyond ordinary circumstances, (like when my computer savvy made the wrong things appear and the right things disappear), causing her to incorporate all of her wits and skills; as scopist, legal transcriptionist, proofreader, editor, and seemingly, a magician, to straighten out my mistakes...all this, and a good lunch, too! She went far and beyond the call of duty for me and my dreams - from the first word to the end results, including editing and book layout.

I will always be appreciative of her, recognizing that all her efforts, as well as her expertise was significant in helping my book become a reality.

I would also like to thank Aunt Shirley who helped provide me with photos and for her recollections of things that escaped me.

This book is lovingly dedicated to my parents, Lila and Samuel Drudge; to my two brothers, Jackne and Nolan Drudge, and to all my family; the ones of my yesterdays; to those of today; and for all those of my tomorrows.

I especially dedicate my book to my children; Charles Brent White, Gregory White, Lorna White Slowikowski, and Nancy White McElfresh. In addition, this legacy is especially for my grandchildren; Christopher White, Erica White Williby, Jonathan White; Brian, Amanda, and Alyssa McElfresh; and Sarah and Hannah Slowikowski; also included, is my only great grandchild, Avery Williby.

I thank my God upon every remembrance of you.

-- Philippians 1:3

719 Francis Street

MY CHILDHOOD

Childhood is the period of life we remember without even trying. It is important to have those memories like a monument, to always remind us of the happy times and unique family experiences.

When we reflect on our past it should be crowded with times we like to relive, over and over again – making us a better person through doing so, because our past automatically becomes a part of the generation that follows.

This phase of life is part of the heritage we bestow through traditions to our children whom we love; that part of us that is immortal. It is a legacy, the most valuable possession a person can give. A part of us that cannot be erased or relived except in memories, and never replaced. Each day must be a day worth remembering, if not one we care to relive, it must not be one we have to forget.

You are invited to join me on my trip down memory lane in 1933 when I was six years old. I lived at 719 Francis Street, Key West, Florida, a neighborhood that is unique in its own right, and a neighborhood like no other on the island.

Our house was located directly across the street from the graveyard, dead center of the island. The landmark is encircled by a tall, iron picket fence that has sharp shafts inset in a concrete foundation. Long ago it had strategically been located for protection from the attacks of pirates who were known to plunder the coastline like the fierce hurricanes that made sudden attacks unannounced.

As a child, I never thought about why the graveyard was there, all I knew was that I lived across a very narrow street and we were neighbors – just as close a neighbor as Mrs. Geneva and her family on the right and old Lucille Borden on the left. The difference was those particular neighbors across the street were more quiet than the others...that's how my family made light of the location.

Towering above the burial ground, to the far left corner, the fire bell could be seen or heard from a great distance. It was a source of much anticipation and entertainment for all the islanders. Its deep, penetrating sound resonated all over the island when a fire alarm was sounded. Suddenly, the town would become like a beehive with everyone swarming in all directions.

There was no way to tell where the fire was, you simply followed the crowd. It became "the main event" where you were part of the audience or became a Good Samaritan. In all the frenzy, a person was seen to throw a piano off the floor of a second-story building. Every fire was a new experience.

If the bell wasn't clanging for a fire, it was tolling the death of a noted personality. Other than that, its measured strokes signaled the nine o'clock curfew. Children less than eighteen years of age caught out after that time were escorted home by the police.

Another time piece on the island was the five o'clock cannon that was set off daily at the old army barracks. This meant different things to different people. To me it meant...GET HOME! Between these two regulations, the town appeared to have all the law and order it needed.

In addition to these timing devices, the barometer was considered the lifeline. It was the islander's best and only means of protection from the killer hurricanes that threatened their shores. It could detect bad weather worsening by the gradual fall of barometric pressure recorded by the instrument. Grandpa Pierce was our weatherman. He always kept a barometer on the wall in the hallway where he could easily monitor the weather on a routine basis. It was his decision, when he felt like life was in the balance, to issue orders for the family to prepare for the worst while they prayed for the best. Needless to say, the homestead always survived, suffering only minor damages at times from the blows that were dealt it.

In sharp contrast to these realities was the illusion of life abounding within that fenced, hallowed ground. This was made possible by the towering Poinciana trees casting comforting silhouettes in all directions. The profusion of color from their orange and red blooms was made more radiant as the glorious sunset tilted in their direction.

Crotons dedicated their exotic shapes and patterns, dotting the landscape with their many varieties along with the imperishable, delicate periwinkles of every hue that were used to form hedges and fill-ins where desired. A feeling of pride and a sense of dedication was always evident.

Eventually, rows of wood framed houses, all aligned side by side, would surround the familiar landmark like a fortress that evokes solidarity; a stronghold that was to become a permanent fixture for future generations. The town had an identity; Cayo Hueso, the Spanish name for Key West.

Some of these houses were brought over from the Bahamas in one piece and some in parts. Others were built in imitation of the Bahamian architecture, giving the

3

island an antiquated appearance. They eventually became known as Conch houses because they were owned by the Conchs, as the natives were called in honor of the famous shelled seafood that is bountiful in the surrounding waters.

The Conch homes were made to last forever. Pa Pierce was always painting and repairing his home, taking great pride in its beauty. It wasn't difficult to keep an old conch house new-looking. Their sturdy structures were especially designed to lean and sway with the ferocious winds of the hurricanes, fastened together by steel rods from the main support to the other or used as an added protection. They were made to last forever through the use of hard sappy pine. Pegs (wood dowels) were used instead of nails by the ship's carpenters who built many of the houses. The sturdy structures, strictly rectangular in design, sport gabled roofs topped with cedar shakes, scuttles and gutters. As the original shingles blew off the roofs, they were replaced with galvanized tin shingles. Tin gutters ran along the eaves to trap rain, the only water supply which was stored in large cement cisterns. Man-sized scuttles protruded from the triangular roofs, resembling a hatch – a direct influence of the ship builders.

Many of the old Conch houses were dressed in elaborate scrolls within a framework of railings. The ornamental designs; gingerbread, pineapple, and fish, were fashioned for the specific purpose of informing people of the background of the household or indicated a profession. One pattern was especially designed to disclose information on an illegal business, the rum-runs that Hemingway wrote about.

Enhancing the beauty further, dormer windows and widow walks, affixed like badges of honor, served as

lookout towers.   Tamarind, sapodilla, Spanish lime,
avocado, and coconut trees loomed like giant umbrellas
around the homes. Appetizing arrays of guava, key lime,
paw-paw (papaya), mango, sea grape, banana, sour sop,
and sugar apple trees formed a colorful and distinctive
background all year round. These homes in future years
would become invaluable antiques.

Welcome to my world at the old homestead at 719
Francis Street where I lived during some of my early
childhood years. The two-story rectangular conch house
was my mother's parents' home where they lived all
their life – Ma and Pa Pierce. I remember it as a place of
refuge, like a beacon emitting signals of love, caring, and
sharing.   It was a place where all family members
returned sooner or later, singly or collectively – many
times. Everyone stayed until they could "get on their feet
again," a familiar saying that indicated no particular time
limit. Actually, when you arrived, you never wanted to
leave.   This home was childhood – the foundation of
many lives.

There isn't anything that gives me more pleasure
than thinking about my childhood. The further away I
get from those days the more automatic it becomes to
want to enter that world and become a child again.   It
comes easy. I find myself reminiscing more often. At
times, without any prompting I find myself skating
down the sidewalks again, leaping over the cracks that
separated the large squares of cement, then leaping over
the curb into the street, up and down the little smooth
ramps that connect the street to the sidewalk.

Cars were scarce in my hometown on the island of
Key West, Florida, the tip end of the U.S.A. The main
mode of transportation was bicycles or legs, so the streets

were safe. Instead of children having to watch for cars, it was the other way around.

The island only measures eight miles long and one mile wide. Some like to think of it as stretching from the Atlantic to the Gulf of Mexico. Others use Duval Street as a measuring device, by referring to it as the world's longest main street - running from the Gulf of Mexico to the Atlantic Ocean. My favorite description in real terms is: it's from the sunrise; where morning dawns, to the sunset; where evening fades...with five minutes travel time (by bike) in between.

Most of the time though, a cue from out of nowhere signals the memory bank; like the smell of bubble gum or a fresh box of crayons, or meeting or hearing about an old friend I haven't seen since we were children together. It causes flashbacks - a unique experience incomparable to any other. One recollection bears memory to the next, mingling so fast they are difficult to grasp. You get a feeling like you're falling into outer space and you need to catch on to something, but it's not there. It's my past; it's part of me, mine and mine alone...till' eternity.

I find a secret, inward pleasure in having something no one else in the world possesses and it can't be bought at any price. It can't be taken away either. If the transmitter ever ceases to function, the recorder will preserve the memorabilia. It's the most valuable and cherished material possession I own - my childhood memories ... my domain. No one can ever enter that realm. My childhood was special and now I realize why. I was allowed to be a child and childhood lasted a long time.

When I think about my childhood it's like a photograph - all there at once. However, the picture is incomplete. It does not portray the brief intervals of my life that was interrupted when my parents moved further up the Keys to follow the jobs. There were many unforgettable and beautiful memories during those times that should be in the background of that original photograph but they're not there. They only appear when I take special care to fill them in. They are a different photograph – one among many but part of my album.

Henceforth, we are essentially a part of impressions – imprints of our past, some greater than others. Certain stages of life definitely leave a greater impression than others. Our behavior is a part of our past. There is no escaping any more than returning.

Most young people don't begin to think about their heritage until they marry and begin to raise a family. Up to that point, everything is taken for granted. Suddenly, the past becomes more and more important with maturity. As young adults they realize what they remember about their childhood is not enough. The roots go deeper. There's a system of taproots that become as important as they are prominent. They realize they are part of the system or mold that makes them what they are today or ever hope to become.

My childhood was like sunshine, living with all the family at my grandparents' home. Ma and Pa Pierce, (Ellen and Charles), had seven children; Lila, the oldest and my beloved mother, Golden, Lewis, Lester, Virginia (Gina), Shirley and Kirkwood (Kirk).

My Ma Pierce was the Rock of the family, constant and steadfast as the sea breezes that fanned the island. She was stocky, but well built in good proportion. Her round face was inset with large, blue eyes and thick eyebrows. Her long, thick brown hair (that reached to her knees) almost over-shadowed the silver threads woven in between. She kept it well groomed with the help of the horse comb (not that it had anything to do with horses.) It became everyone's favorite because the teeth were so far apart it made clearing the knots easier. She was always neatly attired in a cotton print dress covered by a full apron supported by a bib. Her Mona Lisa smile created an aura of complacency and steadfastness, a countenance that never faulted. She lived by her strong convictions and strict upbringing where the Bible was the foundation for living. Her Bible was a permanent fixture in the home she shared so graciously over the years – the cornerstone of her life and loved ones. Known for preaching "where there's a will, there's a way," she used many opportunities to prove her point.

One of the most profound and lasting influences she had on my life was the manner in which she used biblical quotes to admonish anyone and that's all it took to establish peace and understanding. When she spoke...you listened. It was as if God Himself had spoken.

Hand in hand my grandmother and I would walk in the graveyard often to tend the family plot or attend a funeral. It was customary to go to most funerals whether in mourning, to offer sympathy, or out of sheer curiosity. Everyone knew everyone and if they didn't, they knew the next of kin or one of their ancestors somewhere down the line. My Ma Pierce always seemed obligated to show respect, is how she put it, so we didn't miss many as I remember. Some could stand motionless without shedding a tear, but I cried for those. I probably set a world record for "the person who cried at the most funerals." I remember looking from one to the other to see who would break down first. Sometimes, I thought no one ever would and I couldn't understand why. But that didn't stop me. Someone just had to raise a handkerchief or even reach for one and my tears flowed easily and still do. I suppose I had enough practice.

On one particular occasion my grandmother and I headed for the family plot. We entered the small gate across the street and sauntered along the main dirt road as we had done many times before. We had only gone a short distance when I noticed she was in a somber mood. She seemed troubled and sad. I wasn't used to seeing her that way, so I began to read inscriptions aloud, as best as a six year old could do, trying to be some consolation.

I didn't get any response until I tugged on her hand and said, "Look, Ma, Mary Lonely. She must be real lonely, huh, Ma?"

As she looked to her right where I was pointing, she burst into laughter. I thought she would never stop and I laughed right along with her although at the moment I didn't know why. It didn't matter. It was good to see her happy again.

"That's *Maloney*," she gasped as she caught her breath. We stopped long enough for her to teach me a thorough reading lesson and a complete history of the Maloney family too. I didn't care. We were both happy now as we continued on our way.

One of the routes led us past the huge turret with the tall life-sized statue of a sailor holding an oar. It commemorated the loss of hundreds of lives on the American battleship, The Spanish Main, sunk in the nearby Cuban harbor.

Not far was General Abe Sawyer, Key West's own dwarf who gained notoriety as he traveled in many expositions, and upon dying, requested to be buried in a man-sized casket - the desire of his life to gain equality.

We stopped along the way for brief intervals to pass the time of day with various ones. Some visited the gravesites on a daily basis as routine as the weather. It was a time to share feelings and gossip over the trivial.

In all directions you could see heads bobbing up then disappearing as people busied themselves weeding, hedging, and decorating with various plants. The illusion was of life abounding instead of death and darkness.

Squeaky hand pumps at the deep wells here and there broke the silence as people pumped water for their plants. Everyone had to be watchful of the wells that were ground level, camouflaged with over-grown debris. The wells above ground with their red brick designs added a quaint touch of elegance.

After completing all my grandmother had set out to do, we headed home. Little did I realize I had just lived a lifetime within that walk today, because I would carry the experience with me for the rest of my life.

I cherish that unforgettable experience that is ingrained in my memory forever. It never fades. When I walk that same walk now, it's a different season for a different reason and I'm the one that's sad...so now I understand. The experience is like the monument, prominent and as beautiful today as yesterday. I can smile and feel comforted as sadness is overcome with solace.

It wasn't long we were back home again, picking up where we left off.

Many times my grandmother bribed me with a penny to go to the little Cuban store around the corner, Vicente's. His store was the front part of his two story

wood house. Everything was mostly sold by the pound.
Large galvanized cans of flour, rice, grits, potatoes, along
with many others, sat around the room. The candy is
what I remember most. The glass showcase was always
stocked with an array of colorful candies and huge jars of
candy sat on the counter. I have never seen anything like
it before or since. Sometimes, I guess I spent an hour
choosing a one cent piece of candy, because I remember
getting into trouble for taking so long.

Anyway, I never got spanked in my life, because
when I was born (the first), my proud father laid down
the law to all the family in a big oration that I was never
to be spanked. Any discipline would be in the form of a
punishment which was sitting in the corner, and only
two people were qualified to carry that out...my Mother
and my Father. That proclamation was carried out as he
ordered, and henceforth, I was a perfect, unspanked
child all my life.

My Daddy, Samuel Hartford Drudge, was
handsome and big in stature. His tall, straight, muscular
body always exhibited a proud stance, part of which was
the product of his earlier training as a prize fighter in Key
West. He always seemed proud to display the scar from
a broken collarbone he had gotten in the ring. Future
years would hold great successes for him in many fields,
even though he never had any formal education. The
most outstanding accomplishments during his younger
years were as a railroad foreman and when he owned his
own bakery. From then onward, he became a building
contractor and was a construction foreman of the
overseas highway bridges. During this period, he was
also hired to replace many homes along the keys that
were destroyed by a hurricane. He often bragged, "If one
of those homes were ever swept away, nothing in Key

11

West or the Florida Keys would be standing." They're all still there. He always maintained his word was his bond - his guarantee to all who ever knew him.

Among other attributes, he built much of the island in his day; many of the homes and motels that still exist can attest to that. They stand as reminders of how proud his family was of him. That's the way things were and still remain; our treasured memories that will outlast all our tomorrows. Known to be a man of principle, he commanded great respect and admiration from all the family - my mother included.

My mother's sunny disposition made her beautiful and promoted their relationship that lasted through their golden anniversary. Her inborn talents and high ideals afforded her and her family many accomplishments.

She loved music and learned to play the piano well enough to become an inspiration to all three of her children; me and my two brothers, Earl Jackne, and Nolan Hartford. Over time, we became accomplished musicians, using our talents to play and teach several instruments. We in turn, helped mother attain higher levels in the realm of music. She used her abilities to reach goals far beyond her wildest dreams, and devoted the remaining years of her life to teaching piano...all of her grandchildren included. As she grew older, with each new addition, she kept saying how she wanted to live long enough to teach just one more. Her family dealt with destiny by continuing her dream; where she left off, they began. She was music to all who knew her and her songs continue to be sung.

She became my mentor and best friend over our years together. We cared enough to find the time to listen to each other whether on frivolous things or serious matters, and her wisdom never became outdated. She could make crooked places straight with her helpful words, the kind that build up. Mother and I could share the secrets of our hearts and laugh when nothing was funny. We were inseparable, where hardly a day passed when we weren't together, for as long as she lived - eighty two years. All those past years are but as yesterday. There is no such thing as missing her because I keep her near, and she will be with me as long as the sun and moon endures.

Over the years, mother confided in me that she was the reason my father gave up boxing at the time they became engaged. She explained how Grandpa Drudge, my father's dad, after many failed attempts to get him to quit boxing, persuaded her to give my daddy the ultimatum - her or boxing. Pa Drudge and mother had mutual respect and admiration for each other and they shared the same sentiments he was advocating.

Not long after my parents were married, she confessed to daddy and he accepted their alliance wholeheartedly, viewing the conspiracy as an act of love. He probably had an inkling that his father was the instigator all along. After all, ever since he was nine years old, he and his father had batched together at the lighthouse his father had operated off-shore of the Bahamas. By now, they didn't need words to communicate or express their innermost thoughts and feelings. They had been empowered by the sea that spoke its own language which they had learned to decipher long ago.

The sea has a powerful message that runs a full gamut of emotions similar to our very own. It is through observing these elements God has provided for us that we learn to interpret them and then apply them to our own lives. You can sense meaning in the agitation of the outbursts of foam created by the rolling whitecaps as they crash toward the shore; then witness the gradual release of tension in the soft, frothy spurts that cross your brow. At these moments, you and the sea take on a human quality, where your cares can become as flighty as that foam on the surface of the water. The sea spills out its wisdom for all those who seek to understand its message; to interpret for their own personal gain. The sea had become the mediator, between father and son, showing them direction. It had become the anchor of their soul, their strength and refuge...the tie that binds.

When you're near the sea for years, it is as if you become hypnotized into its way of life that reaches deep into the inner core of your soul and spirit. If the day ever comes that you move far away from that sea, there is a part of you that never leaves.

All our family was connected to the sea in one way or the other. There were lighthouse keepers, fishermen and spongers. The sea was a way of life that provided a livelihood that was constant and consistent. Our family had a built in support system...one for all and all for one. That technique seemed to offer a good survival tactic throughout the great depression along with laboring for one dollar a day working for the WPA system. All in all, life continued on as usual with everyone contributing their part.

Sometimes one of us children would be called in from play to take food around the block on Ashe Street to Ma and Pa Kemp. Ma Kemp was blind and Ma Pierce, her daughter, cooked daily for her and Pa Kemp. At times, Pa Kemp walked around the corner to our house, bringing his tin can with a lid (like a casserole), to pick up their food. Pa Pierce fussed Ma Pierce one day for

14

catering to them and fixing such special dishes. Ma Pierce retaliated with a firm, emphatic, "Now you can put that baby to sleep because it won't do you any good to complain about what I do for my parents. I'm going to do for them as long as I have a breath in my body." That was that - forever! I'm certain that statement took all her breath and that was the strongest language you would ever hear from my grandmother.

Ma Pierce took good care of her parents, Martha and John Kemp. They lived in a two story conch house at 710 Ashe Street, just around the corner. It was kept immaculate and all their needs were met. Every week, Shirley and Gina had to take turns scrubbing all the wood floors; in the home, all of the wood planks in the backyard that encircled the cistern, and the outdoor toilet. Re-hanging curtains and dusting were added responsibilities. Their pay for a day's work was twenty five cents.

The two houses were almost back to back, leaving just enough space in between to encourage exploration, an enticement for us children as great as outer space is for man. A mixture of curiosity and imagination went a long way to create excitement and a world of adventure.

Almost daily, when one of us was designated to carry something to Ma and Pa Kemp, Kirk and I usually went together. He was my uncle (only eighteen months older) so we were brought up like brother and sister. We would go directly there by walking on the sidewalk as we circled the block. When two or more of us decided to band together, we took short cuts that involved going through back yards. We had to crawl over wood fences or squeeze through fences with loose boards, fighting off spiders and their creations, along with bugs of every variety. This is where trouble brewed because we would get side tracked. Those shortcuts could be termed longcuts because that's what they became most of the time. Anyway, we gradually went headlong toward our destination with Kirk usually in the lead.

Kirk generally carried a slingshot everywhere he went, with few exceptions. He would take aim at any bird that crossed our path and was an expert marksman, I'm sorry to say.

We could always be assured that some kind of fruit would entice us along the way. We ate whatever we saw birds eat and one of those delicacies grew wild on vines that ran rampant over most of the fences. The fruit was tiny, about the size of a small strawberry, bright orange in color with lots of bright red seeds. They looked like miniature jack-o-lanterns as they dangled from the vines and we stayed long enough to get our fill of the sweet and succulent fruit. Sometimes, we would rob the birds of their treats by pulling a bud off of a hibiscus plant and suck the sweet juice from its' socket.

Besides being a helper, I frequented my great grandparents' home every day because I felt like I belonged there as much as I did at Ma and Pa Pierce's. There were different friends on Ashe Street too, so I was drawn to spend as much time playing in front of their home as I did on Francis Street. I was in and out often.

The biggest attraction for all of us children was the big, vacant lot across the street where we gathered to play baseball hours on end. All the screaming and negotiating created the only source of sound in the neighborhood back then. I was fortunate to have two homes. First and foremost, God's presence prevailed in both. The main difference was in formality. The love and caring was the same.

Now that those childhood days have distanced themselves from me, I find myself comparing my world of today, tomorrow, and beyond, with that of my yesterdays.

Just imagine! Living in a world that is quiet and safe and in the midst of an exotic garden, where every breath you breathe is purified by the salty, ocean breezes as they drift and constantly fan the island. For a small moment, consider how fortunate to have the only water supply distilled as the clouds drop the rain upon the island abundantly.

On a seasonal note, newcomers must be very observant or the seasons will come and go unnoticed because the changes are so subtle...but they exist - the moon says so. It was appointed to create signs and seasons - Key West included. Fortunately, it blessed our island with a gentle and smooth transition from one season to the next, but the tell-tale signs are as plain as day to the ones who count.

Holidays pronounce the seasons with remarkable accuracy. Like the fourth of July that has an explosive way of announcing it's summertime, along with the changeable weather patterns and special blooms that help designate the seasons.

Even more exuberant, the sun seems to stand still in its habitat, making the hot days longer. There, the only relief to be found is in the comfort of the clouds when they hover like a canopy. Best of all, schools are out and most of the tropical fruits are ripe, and that is an indication all the homemade ice cream parlors will be in full swing; making tutti-frutti, sapodilla, coconut, guava, sour sop, sugar apple, and others. The most famous was Knowles ice cream parlor on the corner of Caroline and Margaret streets. He made his business unique by serving the ice cream in thick glasses instead of in fancy dishes. Take it from me, it's a different experience; once tried, it becomes contagious. That landmark became famous and the building has since been moved to a Mallory Square location for exhibition.

As fall approaches, the days begin to be a little shorter and hurricanes become a threat...they confirm the season! However, Halloween and Thanksgiving create refreshing excitement and add variety to life in the tropics.

As winter approaches, the sun begins to rest more, making the days shorter and cooler as the Christmas holidays grow near. You may even be able to wear a light sweater this time of the year.

Spring means more rain and many new blooms with extravagant fragrances. More butterflies are noticeable as they decorate the foliage and kites decorate the sky with their artful displays, and besides, it's the Easter holiday!

In all due respect, up to this point, part of the balancing act has been completed in His seasons of life. From this point of view, Key West has earned its name, Paradise.

Envision: No phones, radios, TVs, computers, or VCRs. No airplanes, ambulances, or sirens...a treasured island in every sense of the word. If you were born there, you were called a Conch and were proud of it. There is no pretense in the feeling that once a Conch...always a Conch...as the saying goes, and the natives will attest to that. All stood ready to defend their beloved island against any riffraff.

To the naked eye, everything appeared as if it was unwound, moving in slow motion. There was no place to go in a hurry and if you had to go somewhere, it only took ten or so minutes to walk anywhere or five or so minutes to ride your bicycle to get there. Besides, there were so many short cuts; everything seemed like just a hop, skip, or a jump away.

Days always seemed long as the hours stretched between daylight and darkness. Without fail, the sun illuminates the island almost instantly as it explodes in the eastern horizon, appearing as if it is coming up from the depths of the Atlantic Ocean...in clear view of the shoreline. From a distance, between dark and daybreak, the graceful palms become as fireworks against the rising sun as it performs its first magical feat of the day by turning the sea of glass into a bed of sparkling diamonds for as far as the eyes can see.

Gradually, as the hours slowly fade away, the sun begins to wane as it repositions itself into the western sky. There, in full view, you can watch the panorama of the sun as it reluctantly begins its descent toward the vast waters of the Gulf of Mexico. It creates a spectacular array of kaleidoscopic changes of color that transform the western sky right before your very eyes - and at close range. You'll see the sun, like a huge ball of fire as it appears to melt into the sea, turning its surroundings into a fiery spectacle before being doused; sinking into its watery resting spot.

The sun rises and the sun sets and hurries back to where it rises. There He has marked out the horizon on the face of the waters for a boundary between light and darkness. Each sunrise and sunset is a new experience that will never be duplicated...once witnessed...never to be forgotten.

The long hours of daylight afforded more time and offered more freedom for children to realize their dreams and future successes. With less demands, they

19

had time to explore...to become a Free Spirit...One that knows right from wrong and taught to be accountable.

Family values took precedence over worldly affairs in the old days. Sunday school and church attendance were our family's only investment for the future. It all seemed rooted in a biblical quote that was preached to us consistently; "Remember the Sabbath day, to keep it holy." It wasn't just a verse to quote, it was a law, one that was practiced within our family and promoted in our community. All businesses had to remain closed on Sundays. Even the children seemed to disappear. We were told, in no uncertain terms, "There will be no running wild and loud carrying on...this is the Lord's Day."

I can still hear that command in the form of guilt when I go against the grain - disobedient to the Word that was instilled in me as a child, meant for all time. It's as if the Ten Commandments have become suspect in today's world, where the unaccepted has become accepted. These are the new times and those were the old times, but the Sabbath is the Lord's time...I was taught to believe. I wish the "old times" could be the "now times." Some things must and should change - for the better; others can be improved upon; but there are many things that should never change.

Our Sundays didn't just begin on Sunday - all week long there were preparations being made for that special day, which included the food; even the kitchen rested on the Sabbath. There were special clothes designated for Sundays only and they all took on that name...shoes became Sunday school shoes...all articles of clothing for that day, had its name tag. When all the Sunday clothes were outgrown or became worn, they took on a new identity - school clothes.

At 9:30 a.m. on Sunday morning, we went to Sunday school at the First Congregational Church, 527 William Street, where the family attended for generations. On every special occasion, the leaders devoted lots of time and effort practicing with the children for programs to help them make the Bible stories come alive, through recitations, songs, and realistic costumes. Everyone looked forward to the productions. At the end of each year, for the Christmas program, a giant Christmas tree, in its entire splendor, stood before the pews, near the altar, in celebration of the great event. Under the tree, for every child, was a five pound brown paper bag loaded with fruit, nuts, a box of chocolates, along with a special gift from each one's Sunday school teacher. How special can special be! I've often pondered why they are the only Christmas tree experiences I've never forgotten.

At 4:00 p.m. that same day, all of us children had to go to Sunday school again, with Ma Pierce, at the Church of God. Their children's programs were extravagant and worthwhile, too, affording us many memorable times. The church was only two blocks to the left of our house, which is Olivia Street. Turning right on that narrow street, mid-way the block, sits the small church facing the nearby graves that could easily be considered part of the congregation. It was known as the Holy Roller Church. There's a lot of history behind that rambunctious church. It was a gathering spot at night for the members as well as for the spectators. Some of my family took me along at times to stand outside where the crowds gathered. Some appeared as curious onlookers, while others used the opportunity to meet friends, but there were many who felt they could receive a spiritual blessing and inspiration by attending the gathering.

Their music was spirited, evoking many emotions from all who gathered; crying, shouting, clapping and stomping with the loud music. Everyone became involved. There was always a display of jubilation by the raising of arms as inspiring hymns were belted out, like: Count Your Blessings, Name Them One by One; When We All Get to Heaven; and another favorite, In the Sweet Bye and Bye. All the hymns they sung reflected their deepest convictions.

Opposite Olivia Street, on the other side of the graveyard, is the graveyard alley, a little paved road that helps complete the circle.

About six blocks to the right of the gates is the Gulf of Mexico, where wharves, shipyards and strings of dinghies lined the shore. Turtle Krawls and fish markets were always in competition with sponge markets to see which could out-stink the other. Whiffs of the odors intermingled with the smell of grits and grunts that were the mainstay of many Key Westers' diet.

In those days, most families automatically became thrifty and industrious, without realizing the transformation. Making the most of what you had and being thankful at the same time was happiness. After everyone's needs were met and tasks were completed, a "Let the Rest of the World Go By" mentality took over.

The seemingly endless days never found me bored. I could always entertain myself at Ma and Pa Kemp's house. It was always exciting to explore and a fun adventure. Every time was a new experience.

Their home had a porch all across the front that almost touched the sidewalk. It was all enclosed by railings except at the left end where three small, cement steps led up to the porch. I played by myself on those steps many times, jumping and alternating my feet up and down, over and over and concocting a form of hopscotch for one, that I made up as I went along.

A large trunk, used for Pa Kemp's tools, was a permanent fixture at the far right end, along with the towering avocado tree that shaded most of the home.

The entrance door was in the middle, but no one could use that door except the church people who came every week with the minister for worship and song. There were designated areas that were excluded to many, which included me. Maybe that's what aroused my curiosity to probe and investigate every nook and cranny.

A narrow cement walkway ran along the left side of the home which led to the side entrance at the far back, where Ma and Pa Kemp always sat facing each other on opposite sides of the doorway, which remained open all day. His favorite chair was a big cane rocker where he could be found puffing on a corncob pipe occasionally or nodding in and out during the day. She was always neatly cuddled in a small cushioned rocker, attired in a full-length cotton print dress and soft felt Indian moccasins on her tiny feet. The height of their day came when Pa Kemp read the Bible to her and they studied the Word together.

On entering that room, the first thing that catches your attention is a large, round mahogany table with a tall kerosene lamp in the middle and an over-sized Bible nearby. Lace curtains dressed the windows along the back wall. On the opposite wall was a huge grandfather clock that tick-tocked relentlessly. Nearby, was a double chiffonier with many drawers. There was a place for everything but there was only one thing that enticed me...church envelopes! They were always in the top center drawer. I had never seen anything like them

23

before. I suppose they seemed to me like little purses to stash secret things in. I don't know why they drew me like a magnet.

I would tip toe quietly after making sure they were both nodding and then go into action. I was determined to get a few of those envelopes. Sometimes I could manage to open that drawer without a squeak, but I overlooked the fact that even though Ma Kemp was blind, her hearing was good enough for both of them. I always got caught at one stage or the other, but only after making a mess for Pa Kemp to straighten out while he grunted and groaned, but that never stopped me from trying again. Ma Pierce jarred my mind many times as to staying out of that drawer. Sometimes I heeded. Other times her advice fell on deaf ears. All I know is on entering that room I felt like Alice in Wonderland but after taking a few steps, approaching that chiffonier, a Dick Tracy Syndrome overtook me. I was intent on discovering all that was forbidden.

Regardless of how many times I entered their home, it was as if for the first time. Everything always remained the same but my investigative powers were not convinced. I could always find something I never saw before. I had a perpetual curiosity that could not ever be satisfied.

I am convinced today, if I could re-enter that world again, I'd still peer in at those envelopes and even though I'd see them in a different light, I could reconcile the difference.

When I touch my church envelopes that look the same today as then, I have to smile and ponder the difference. That can't happen unless I re-enter that child's world again...and so I do.

Almost as big a temptation to lure me as the church envelopes, was a box of social tea crackers. They were always in Pa Kemp's full view from the sitting room, on top of a small corner cabinet in the kitchen, to the right, just inside the doorway. They were Ma Kemp's favorites, served with her hot tea everyday, so Pa Kemp kept close watch in that direction.

Sometimes I was guilty of helping myself and when caught in the act, I was reminded that times were "hard to come by." Sometimes he would mete out one and sometimes none and in that case I would beg for a penny. At this point, I would get a lecture as to the scarcity of money while his large hands, unsteady as a flickering wick in the old oil lamp, fumbled in his pocket to pull out a little leather change purse. I remember the two little knobs that had to be twisted in opposite directions in order to be opened. I can see it as clear today as yesterday...his large fingers, trembling, as he dug deep enough to reach the tiny coin.

I'll never realize the sacrifice involved in the hundreds of times we shared those moments over time, but I do know, more than anyone else can ever know, how much wealth can be created by a penny. It's all in remembering that creates the true value and it can't be figured in dollars and cents because there is greater joy to be found in reliving memories than what we experienced at the time we lived them.

I refuse to let go of those memories. Until this day, I keep a replica of that change purse in my pocketbook that goes everywhere I go. It's not because I need a reminder. It's like winning a medal...the award is forever. Every time I use my change purse, it gives me a sense of belonging to someone who still belongs to me.

There were numerous opportunities that presented themselves for me to interact in my great grandparents' lives throughout my childhood; however, I must admit many of those were directly related to my busybody status. That could be blamed on my great imagination and inquisitive nature which created many roles for me to play as a child. I could concoct any scene that suited my fancy at the time to entertain myself, and they could always have a happy ending because I was in control. So I followed my instincts in all that fascinated me, for as long as I could remember, sneaking and prying, covering as much ground as I could until I was stopped in my tracks. At that time, a little impromptu speech would follow as gentle gestures ushered me into the right direction.

Sometimes a clue from out of nowhere would prompt me into action. One such occasion came when the smell of bay rum and moth balls drifted in my direction. The scents appeared to come from the hallway that led to the front door. It was just around the corner from the sitting room.

I followed my nose which led me to their bedroom that was directly inside the hall and on the left. I knew that room was off limits to me but I ventured in anyway. The quiet atmosphere almost seemed eerie, making me feel apprehensive with the prospect of getting caught in places I didn't belong.

On entering the big room, on the left was a wash stand that held a gorgeous porcelain basin with a pitcher to match. Next to that furniture was a portable clothes closet and on the opposite wall, a huge chest of drawers. In between that setting was a large bed, beautifully decorated in harmony with all the furnishings. The room appeared like a sanctuary, so spacious and immaculate.

Windows, all along the outer wall, were usually open, allowing air to circulate and freshen the room. There were just enough puffs to give life to the delicate curtains that decorated the windows.

On leaving, if I went out the same door where I had entered their bedroom, on the left, a flight of stairs led to the upstairs where two bedrooms were always ready for any guest, mainly, a son or grandsons who visited occasionally.

On returning to the downstairs area, directly across the hall from their bedroom, was the parlor; a large, rectangular room, specifically designated for church services. It was very spacious and accommodating. There were several windows; all decorated with lace and slatted shutters that gave privacy and could filter out the sun where desired.

A carpet of tapestry with designs covered most of the wood floor, giving the room a regal appearance. Matching sets of white wicker furniture framed the picture to perfection.

Nothing ever changed that room...there was no reason to. It was a specific space devoted for a specific purpose, like a memorial or altar. It took on a human quality that lived and breathed traditions and beliefs like the family who lived there all their life. That parlor has remained like a beacon in my life, flashing signals that guide and direct my paths. It is a testimony that I have taken as a part of my inheritance forever.

I never stayed long in that room at any one time because I felt out of place there, but I knew I'd be back again, many times over.

Little did I realize at that time, the foundation of my life was being built and would remain a permanent part of my world until the end of time. The further I've grown from those days the more I've found myself wanting to return. There is no substitute or replacement for the moments shared back then; like precious stones, they become more valuable with age.

Looking back to my earlier years, I remember my great grandparents, Ma and Pa Kemp, as heirlooms and I was the heir, reaping all the benefits of my inheritance while in the midst of my life. Their compassion and understanding were always reflected in their soft words that were fitly spoken and seemed destined for a little girl just like me. They had lost their three year old daughter, years before, who became ill, died, and was buried while her father (Pa Kemp) was earning his living at sea on a fishing trip. It devastated them, and almost killed Pa Kemp. Perhaps, in the imagination of their hearts, I had become their little girl. I will carry them both with me the rest of my life and into eternity.

I refuse to cease remembering all that I'm allowed, for I am satisfied to know, the ones I do remember are of such value, they more than compensate for what little may have escaped me.

There is nothing can take the place of the family. The family is life. It's like a human being; if you lose a member of the body, it creates a weakness that can not be replaced by another of its kind. Where there's family unity, there's strength. One must compensate for the other to establish balance and harmony. A structured family offers a sanctuary against all odds. A disjointed family becomes incomplete. It has the same effect as beginning a movie, getting disturbed in the middle, then returning at the end. You've not just lost lots of the action, but the sum and substance as well. There must be an "all for one and one for all" mentality...the survival tactic put into action during the great depression.

In my treasure chest of childhood memories, the most prominent and meaningful possession I find is the value of living within a family where everything always seemed to remain the same. It gave my life a feeling of permanency - as if carved in stone.

Our neighborhood was like a family, usually peaceful, where you could count on seeing everyone leisurely rocking or swinging to and fro on their front porch, every night of the week as well as in the day. It was a place you could think your own thoughts and at times share a few.

The big wood-slatted double-seated swing hanging by chains from the rafters on the broad front porch was a gathering spot for the children as well as for the adults. It was a place where dreams and fantasies, like making kites, originated and became realities in my world. That's where Kirk comes into the picture.

He was a dark, curly-haired brunette of ordinary build and size and was an expert kite maker. He was my idol and my hero. There wasn't anything Kirk couldn't do. He led and I followed ... most of the time.

Kirk took great pains with his kite making techniques. I remember holding the tissue paper while he cut out the designs, squares, and all the angles. Then I would hold the sticks he had chipped from old boards while he tied them together with thread and pasted on the paper. Everything was made from discarded scraps, and the paste was a mixture of flour and water. Sometimes he'd make fancy frills for the edges from rags and newspapers and always had a long, long tail made from an old sheet cut in narrow strips. Tails varied according to the size of the kite.

The boys of the neighborhood would hold kite contests. Some kites would be judged according to how deep it could dive and pull out of the spin or how it could stand still and execute graceful dips and turns, then return to a still position. The beauty was also considered part of the competition. Kite fights were lots of fun to watch too. At times, Kirk would pull his kite down during the preliminaries to take some of the cloth tail off. He seemed to always know what it needed to make it perform as a winner. Kite making was an art. I used to like the newspaper kites the most. Bits and pieces of discarded, colored tissue paper and wrappings were used with great ingenuity to make insets and to form patterns.

Once in awhile a big kite would take a sudden spiral downward with a big burst of wind. Suddenly, a big statue in the catholic cemetery was wearing a frilly hat – at least it appeared that way and after much laughter, Kirk would jump the fence to retrieve what was left of his masterpiece.

My part of the kite-making expedition involved holding things in place while the procedures were going on and holding the kite up as high as I could reach while Kirk was at the other end of a long line running to launch it. We won most of the kite contests through skill and ingenuity and when that didn't work, bluffing did (Kirk was known for his prowess and downright out fighting skills.) Everyone respected him – even me.

It was such fun to watch Kirk in a big game of marbles, too. He was an expert. A gang of boys would gather in the back yard where there was lots of firm dirt. After drawing the circle that held the marbles, they took turns throwing their taw up to guts, a line about the distance of five or six feet from the circle. The player nearest to the line went first and then on according to rank. I've witnessed many scrimmages over big debates on whose marble was the closest to that line (after a toe or two aided the toss.) I remember the fights more then the games. Each play seemed to bring dissension. I suppose all those boys today would agree with me when I say the arguments and fights were more fun than the games.

Playing marbles could become very involved. Choosing which kind of marble would be allowed as a taw and deciding on the rules that would apply to the particular game, were only some of the compromises that had to be reached. Little steelies, like ball bearings, were used often as taws. At times, larger ones were used but if one used a steely, all used a steely and of the same size. The boys would take great pride in splitting any of the marbles in the circle or on the outside, as well. It wasn't easy but brought higher stakes. Rules were invented along the way like being allowed to change your taw during the game for your good luck taw. There was no end to all the improvisations.

I was only allowed to play marbles with a certain group, where Kirk could bend the rules a little. I was allowed to "poke," which is pushing the hand forward along with the marble that made it go with more force. I'd miss lots of times but Kirk would assure me not to worry – he'd make up for the losses. Dozens of large fruitcake cans loaded with every conceivable size and color marble imaginable stored in the upstairs could attest to that remark.

Every once in awhile, when we couldn't find anything in particular to do, we'd visit those cans of marbles. We would peer into those cans for hours, fumbling and admiring each and every one as if they were precious stones.

When there was an abundance of idleness, it bred contempt. Anytime Kirk couldn't think of anything to do, he resorted to catching lizards to throw on me. I was mortified with the prospect while he thought it was funny.

On one occasion (and only one) it became a disaster. Just as he was reaching his hand through a fence to catch his prey, I tried beating him to the draw by throwing a big rock in the lizard's direction in hopes to scare him away, but instead, I caught one of Kirk's fingers, causing his nail to remain pleated for life. He screamed and cried that day while I hurt even more. There was never any animosity between us over the accident; we both saw it for what it was. Over the years, every time we met, he showed me that finger, in jest, as he said, "Remember?" We'd share smiles of regret...it was one ugly memory we wish we could erase, but sometimes it's harder to forget than to remember. However, within moments, it's as if we used that incident as an introduction to some beautiful, fun memories that we never got tired of sharing...they far surpassed the other kind. .

Speaking of another ugly memory, one appeared out of the blue one day when Aunt Gina announced she was going to have the big Spanish lime tree in the front yard cut down. Kirk immediately became belligerent, to say the least. I admired him for his spunk, and encouraged him, as usual.

Everyone loved the tree - it was the mess it created, along with the cleanups that were brought to bear. Passersby and unknowns, all played a role in those details. Pulling the limbs down to reach the fruit junked the small front yard with leaves and debris, along with some pits and skins that would get strewn in every direction as the luscious fruit was eaten. Our Spanish limes were juicy and meaty, unlike other fruit trees that differ from one to the other. Some of the pulp is softer and sweeter; some are bigger than others and some are twins, but all are delicious and they all stain and ruin any clothes the juice touches. Nothing can remove the dark, brown stain. During the season, we were made to wear old play clothes for such occasions.

When all the fruit at the lower levels of the tree were gone, Kirk found an easy solution for reaching the fruit at the top. His ingenuity could work miracles. He would climb out of the upstairs front window, onto the roof where he could reach a limb to enter the tree at that level. I shudder to think of all that could have happened the hundreds of times I watched him accomplish that feat. He'd gather bunches and throw them down for me to try to catch.

Eventually, Gina had her way with the tree, and Kirk, without a doubt, made her regret that decision many times over. He tormented her in one way or the other - until remembrances, like ashes, go away like the tree, carrying a part of us with it. But a link to the past in the chain of happy childhood memories had been broken and could never be replaced, except by putting ourselves in a position of remembrance.

Days always seemed long in the tropics and yet we hated to see each one end. We practically lived outdoors. The good weather allowed us this privilege. A huge sapodilla tree in the back yard along the fence line shaded most of the back yard. Between that sapodilla tree and the giant Spanish lime tree in the middle of the front yard, most of the house and yard were protected from the sun. These trees were always loaded with fruit enticing us by the hour. Sometimes I feel like I was more monkey than human when I reflect back on those times. The sapodilla tree not only gave us all the fruit we wanted but provided us with all the gum we wanted, too. We would get the axe, chip the bark and the sap that flowed was a delicious gum. That was a daily experience. The only drawback was you couldn't blow bubbles with it.

Tropical fruit trees were in abundance everywhere but we didn't have to climb all of them in order to reach the fruit. We would get sticks or rocks to knock them down. Key limes, guava, avocado, banana, coconut, sugar apples, papayas, Spanish limes and sour oranges surrounded the house. If we wanted almonds or tamarinds we had to go a few blocks down the road.

Most of these fruits were used in our "cut-ups." Almost daily many of the neighborhood children would decide to have a cut-up which involved each child bringing one item of fruit or vegetable which was cut up in a large bowl with salt and pepper and old sour (aged lime juice and salt) to garnish. The usual ingredients were raw potatoes, onions, guavas, papayas, limes, apples, oranges, tangerines, sour oranges, lettuce, tomatoes, and carrots. Each child would take turns picking a piece at a time (the leader selected) until all was gone. Then all of us took turns passing the bowl to sip the remaining juices – germs and all. This concoction was usually a weekly experience that became a top priority in our lives, taking the place of candy and goodies of all kinds that were not available to us.

The only problem we encountered with fruit was in eating green guavas that gave us constipation or fever or both - at least they got the blame. The remedies were either a dose of castor oil or citrate of magnesia (that looked like sprite or bubble up.) Until this day, I can't stand to drink any white sodas because of the association. For the fever, a poultice made from the castor oil plant (that grew wild), combined with some balm, was wrapped around the feet - the premise was to draw the heat, far away from the head. Between castor oil (that some people gave their children on a weekly basis as a preventive measure), citrate of magnesia, Vicks salve, and camphorated oil; many symptoms appeared to become less symptomatic - whether in truth or in pretense. When those cures couldn't conquer, aloe (from the aloe plants that grew wild), black salve and other homemade remedies came to the rescue.

For more serious illnesses, doctors were on call to come to the home. For an emergency, a designated room was always prepared and equipped with necessities - like the matching porcelain basin and pitcher along with a slop jar. That room could handle anything from birth to death. The room was kept immaculate and decorative with matching linens and scarves edged with crochet that announced a prominent visitor would be arriving. All year long it was customary to be gathering special items to be set aside in drawers, in preparation for the day when a doctor had to call.

There was always something to keep us busy. We created our own world with very little disturbance from adults. We could feel free for hours at a time, either playing in groups or alone in a make-believe world. My private world was playing doll house. My dolls were real live babies and I took good care of my family. One day continued to the next in my doll's lives like a serial, unfolding one day at a time. I named one Peggy, one Nellie, and one Betsy (a Betsy Wetsy doll, popular at that time.) They were the ones who shared my private world. When I was allowed to buy something, it was a pair of shoes with the little laces and skates or a piece of clothing for my dolls. I had lots of practice being a mother long before motherhood. When I really reached motherhood, I felt as though I had had extensive training in the field.

I always kept my paper doll families too. Each family and their clothes were kept in separate shoe boxes. Some of the paper dolls were bought, like Shirley Temple, who was my favorite. But I would make extra families out of the Sears catalog, cutting out women, men, and children, then matching clothes and accessories to complete housekeeping. I prized my collections as if they lived and breathed.

The outside is where we lived most of the time though, drawing us like magnets to enjoy to the fullest. Dodge ball, baseball, hopscotch, jack stones, bean bags (made with the beans out of the long brown pods of the Poinciana trees), hide and seek, double Dutch jump rope, and egg-crate cart races...all found their way into my life.

The egg-crate cart left me with the greatest impression. I'm fortunate that's all I was left with when I reflect back on the daring episodes. The cart was made sturdy with a support underneath. There were short wood supports across the front and back that had small axles to support the small tires or wheels (at times, skate wheels.) The front axle could swivel and a rope was attached on each side that led to the rider's hands that steered the contraption. The faster Kirk pushed me the louder I would scream for him to stop, but he kept laughing and going faster with his dare-devil tactics. I would become frightened and jerk the rope that ended in many crashes that left me with skinned body parts. Sometimes he would give me a nice, calm ride and we'd take turns, but I was never assured of the outcome. Regardless, I could always be persuaded to try again.

As a general rule, life seemed to flow smoothly from one day to the next. Children in our family seemed to make every day fun. Holidays were extra special...like Valentine's Day. We devoted a lot of thought and planning weeks in advance on projects for the occasion. Every evening we'd encircle the big, round dining room table, cutting out valentines of our own inventions. Many patterns and designs were created with colored paper folded in many layers and cut in various angles, and when opened, looked fancy as lace. Concocting verses (some naughty, some nice) and deciding which to send to whom, took much consideration. We shared laughter and each others' ideas in everything we did.

The smell of crayons, the snip, snip of the scissors, the chit chat and teasing, mixed with the laughter, the decision making; all formulate a picture worth far more to all of us children than a painting of the Mona Lisa...the difference is in the value; one is priceless, the other money can buy.

Halloween was another adventure where the unexpected was always expected. To us, Halloween meant tricks without treats. There were no rewards unless you count punishment as one which only happened occasionally when we were caught... like the day we were cutting costumes and Ma Pierce's cherished table cover fell on opposite sides of the dining room table.

When children have to improvise with every detail, it's amazing how young minds respond. There was no end to the ingenuity involved. Costumes presented a big challenge but lots of fun. Old stockings and discarded clothing, bed ware and remnants, combined with imagination, created costumes that could never be duplicated. Paper masks took lots of time and patience and contriving all the tricks we would pull, along with who would be at the receiving end of those plots, was no easy feat. Kirk masterminded the operation.

I remember one in particular. Kirk wrapped a rock in a piece of cloth with a long string attached. The plan was to sneak up to the front door of someone we wanted to tease and swing the rock to knock, then run as fast as we could to hide where we could see their reaction to our prank. That's all Halloween meant to us in those days – that's all anyone expected.

All holidays were homemade holidays; Christmas was no exception. The season began with the baking of fruit cakes - they were Christmas. Even the tree was a home grown pine that was cut down from somewhere on the island and decorated with hand made ornaments, like the colored paper chains that were made in school. They were the decorations that I remember most. I'm sure it's because some of them were a part of me - a little circle within chains of circles that linked me to an old time family memory of long ago. Everyone played some role in making the tree more than just a Christmas tree - it was a tree of life; a living example of gifts that only a family can appreciate and share with one another.

Playing in the rain was as much a part of my childhood as the holidays and going to church and Sunday school. Almost every time it rained (and that was often in the tropics), we zoomed into the house to put on old clothes so we could go play in the rain. Usually, there was a gutter running along the eave of the gabled roof that was disconnected and torrents of water would pour in a big, steady stream which seemed like a waterfall to us. We'd take turns standing under the flow, then run through it screaming and yelling our lungs out, enjoying the pounding on our small bodies. The rain water was always cold and enticing.

Pa Pierce didn't leave a gutter loose for very long though, because that was our only source of water which emptied into the large cement cistern in the back yard. If we didn't have the gutter, we had the puddles along the sidewalk where we sailed boats made of leaves or sticks. The most joy was in feeling the stinging rain on our bodies.

Rainy nights were magical too, lying in the roomy upstairs and listening to the rain pelt the tin roof. That has to be the greatest form of magic. Each droplet seems magnified and musical. As the rain begins to dwindle, each raindrop joins the next, forming syncopated rhythms that no orchestra on earth could duplicate. Even the most gullible would be hypnotized.

All of the children slept in the big upstairs. Beds were aligned and a couple of drapes separated a few. The scuttles were opened wide where we could see the heavens above us. The fresh drifting breezes found their way through the openings and fanned us all night long.

No longer had we gotten in bed, Kirk would begin his antics, making us all laugh so hard, sleep didn't have a chance.

I'll always remember his favorite standby; a song, "Said a green little leaf." The song went like this:

> Said a green little leaf
> To a bird flitting by
> Won't you please tell me how
> That you manage to fly...

I never heard that song before Kirk sang it and I haven't heard it since. I have no idea where he learned it. I wish I did. All I know, when I think or talk about that song, it stirs as much emotion within me as when I hear The Star Spangled Banner or America the Beautiful. A flood of unforgettable emotions saturate my soul.

Kirk would go on and on with the song with lots of impromptu and lots of renditions as the laughter continued. As he warmed up and his audience became more receptive, he played the mouth organ. That went on until orders came from below to quiet down. Giggles and varying coughs, choking sounds, grunts, and odd noises of all descriptions drifted gradually away with night as we giggled ourselves to sleep with the playful stars. Some nights were too beautiful to close your eyes. Those memories I will carry with me for the rest of my life because they were the kind of memories that are made to last.

It was on one of these mornings about 5:00 a.m., we were suddenly awakened by an earth shattering explosion that rattled the rafters. It vibrated the entire island. We were dumb with silence. Everyone thought that the world was coming to an end. It was discovered that old Mr. Karl Von Cosel had blown up his lover's mausoleum across the street directly in front of our house!

We remembered him visiting the above-ground burial vault almost daily for a long period of time. He was a tall, straight-backed man with a proud walk and always dressed in black and white and carried an umbrella.

At Christmastime, he decorated a tree in the vault for his lover. It was believed he even spent some nights in the vault. All the family speculated but failed to draw any conclusion.

It was really a love story. Karl Von Cosel, a Russian, about sixty years old, an x-ray technician and inventor, worked in a hospital where he fell in love with a twenty year old nurse, Elana Hoyos Mesa. Shortly after their meeting, Elana became stricken with tuberculosis and died and was entombed in the cemetery across from our house. He was devastated and eventually removed her body from the graveyard to his home, with the dream of restoring her to life. The macabre story of love beyond the grave was unraveled after police discovered her body, seven years dead, dressed in a wedding gown well preserved in bed and in his home. Von Cosel was charged with illegally exhuming a body, but the statute of limitations prevented prosecution and he was released. He subsequently moved to Zephyrhills, Florida, where he earned a modest living selling postcards of the dead girl and writing for pulp magazines. The story is still a topic of many conversations.

Life soon settled back into a regular rigmarole. We picked up where we left off, playing baseball and dodge ball around the block on Ashe Street in a big vacant lot. When our ball would go over the fence into an old lady's yard, she would not allow us to get it and wouldn't give it back. In those days, buying a ball was almost impossible.

The gang would play awful tricks on that lady. When I reflect back on many incidents involving that woman, it's strange I don't remember ever seeing her. Even when visiting my great grandparents, Ma and Pa Kemp who lived across the street from her, I never saw the woman enter her porch even though everyone else within blocks is still familiar to me. In time, we gradually worked out an amicable solution and our ball games took on a new meaning.

Ashe Street lured us more than Francis Street because it offered us larger and safer areas to play; besides, there were more children to share with.

Francis Street was a main street that almost everyone had to use at various times, including funeral processions, because it had the only gated entrance for vehicles.

Alongside that main gate was a small gate for pedestrians. On entering down the long, main dirt road, to the opposite side of the graveyard, are exit gates to Windsor Lane. This path made it a short cut for anyone to get from one section of the town to the other...so the inevitable happened. It became a busy thoroughfare. All you had to do to reach downtown Key West (Duval Street) was to climb Solares Hill, the highest point on the island. Let me assure you, no mountain-climbing gear is needed for that feat.

Occasionally, an old man clip-clopped by in his shabby horse-drawn wagon. Every one of us would chase and scream at him, "Killie the Horse" until he swiped (or pretended to swipe) his whip at us in anger. Some of us were brave enough to run and catch onto the back of his wagon for a free ride until he raised his whip again.

He was accused of whipping a horse to death and we weren't about to let him forget it. If the truth be known, we were simply looking for excitement and a free ride to boot. Whether he was guilty as accused, I never did know. It didn't matter back then. It gave us a little harmless variation in the course of a day.

Another welcomed sight to the neighborhood was the colored peddlers that could be heard sing-songing their wares in the distance.

Hurray Spanish limes
And we got 'em sweet
Just like a piece
of turkey meat.

The boys were in pairs holding a broomstick at each end with bunches of the scrumptious fruit strung in rows. They were a welcomed sight every year.

In contrast to these street scenes, the one heralding the most attraction was the colored funerals – Mini Mardi Gras.

The police force in full regalia and the big brass band led the procession to the burial ground. The mourners swayed in slow, distinct rhythms, their bodies slumped in solemn resignation as the band played "Swing Low, Sweet Chariot." Many times, some of our family followed the procession to the burial ground.

After the body was committed to the grave, the band struck up, "When the Saints Go Marching In," and there was much jubilation. The pageantry displayed in the celebration seemed to be a combination of jitterbug, hard rock, and the Cuban Fandango. It was as entertaining and interesting as The Greatest Show on Earth. Their customs were a big part of the island's heritage.

I never realized the seriousness of the times because "the more the merrier" attitude prevailed as all the families gathered under one roof. It seemed like a joyous occasion to me. Adults never discussed matters in front of the children, so it was difficult to detect anything awry. I remember sullen expressions and a few tears at times that made me wonder about things I knew better then to ask about. I had cause to watch and wonder, but they were only fleeting moments. In later years, my mother relived all those hard times of the depression for me...in three dimensions.

We cried together as the story unfolded. Some tears were shed, as I realized for the first time, the extreme sacrifices and suffering that were encountered for survival. Some were shed as the natural course of events evolved. I could feel the hunger pains for the first time and hear the cries of the younger children who needed milk; even breast milk had dried up due to the lack of proper nourishment at times. Back then, some new mothers who had an over-abundance of breast milk nursed other babies who couldn't be provided for. Sharing and caring was a sign of the times. However, some of the tears that welled up and overflowed were happy tears in celebration of a family who could unite in spirit in the face of adversity - a family who exhibited faith, steadfastness, and perseverance that never faded away.

My mother explained in great detail how all resources were pooled together, which included talents, ideas, and the decision making process. Everyone had a role to play and exhibited willingness to do more than their share. It wasn't a tit-for-tat game. The women divided all the household chores between them in order to meet the needs of everyone in the family.

There was no such thing as conveniences. The women took turns washing clothes that were performed on a wash board in a big, galvanized tub in the back yard. Sometimes a fire was lit under the tub to boil the clothes as the soil was poked and prodded out of them

44

with a stick. At times, well-water (that couldn't be drank) from the nearby pump in the back yard, was used for washing and rinsing and other chores. Clotheslines were strung all over the back yard where the clothes were hung to dry. Sometimes sheets were strung up for privacy during bath time in the yard. Other than that, baths were gotten upstairs where water had to be hauled and then emptied. The back yard was also a place where some family members washed their hair after a rain shower had filled buckets specifically for that purpose. The pure rain water was known to be healthy and make your hair silky and shiny. This practice continued for many years to come.

Over and beyond these rituals, specific talents came into play that helped promote everyone's welfare. Unforeseen ideas surfaced as if rallying to the cause.

All the women could sew, crochet, or tat. Ma Pierce and Aunt Golden were good seamstresses and made all the clothes, including the undergarments for everyone. All the women could crochet, so at times, they pooled their resources to make crochet bedspreads to raffle, which added to the income. In addition, they made children's crochet dresses and various sizes and designs of edgings for pillow cases that became a popular item of the day.

My mother was the only one who could tat. Tatting required lots of patience because it was very tedious weaving the fine, silky threads in and out with a tiny shuttle. Tatting baby caps and booties to match was like her trademark and became a lifelong legacy to her family. She also designed delicate edgings that made plain clothes fancy.

Any free time was spent rocking on the front porch but always with a lap loaded with needlework;

weaving and designing a masterpiece - their most enjoyable luxury.

It was difficult to determine what went the fastest; the feet, pedaling the treadle on the old singer sewing machine or the fingers hooking and crooking beautiful patterns and designs with the threads.

All the men left home early every morning, going in different directions to try to find work...any job would do. Even Pa Pierce would take off on his bicycle, looking for a job. It was well-established to all concerned; he would never borrow a penny on the homestead "for fear of losing the roof on his children's heads." He set that principle and he lived by it for better or worse.

All the women would anxiously wait as the men returned, one by one, to learn the verdict of the spoils that day. My dad found a job for the WPA digging ditches for one dollar a day and considered himself rich for as long as it lasted. At times there was no income but anything at all was turned over to Ma Pierce, the head of the house, to disburse as best she could.

The women grouped together daily to address the ever-changing situation. Their main concern was deciding on what food they could afford to buy that could be stretched the farthest in order to feed the multitude.

Everyone took turns in the preparation of the meals and the cleanups, in the kitchen and in the home. "Cleanliness is next to Godliness," you could sometimes hear Ma Pierce prompting in the background at the least sign of dissension... usually involving the menial tasks. In short order, everything would be running like clockwork again.

Most of the time the homestead smelled of good things to eat, however limited, but with one exception;

when the cupboard was bare. Anyone could easily be disillusioned if they judged the sum and substance by the tantalizing aromas that hovered in the air from one meal to the next. Food was one area where they could accomplish miracles by making small things do big things - like with fish, where there was usually an ample supply. It was the one food that had a beginning but no ending. It was steamed, stewed, boiled, baked, made into chowder and cakes, or combined in so many ways with so many things…at times, stretched so far, it lost its elasticity; camouflaged beyond recognition. Fish had become one of the main staples because we had a commercial fisherman in the family, Uncle Johnnie, Aunt Golden's husband.

Henceforth, fish dominated many of the menus, to such an extent, as time went by, we equated fish with being poor and wished we could squelch the odor to make us less conspicuous in the neighborhood.

All the women were good cooks and could come up with lots of good concoctions. The main one (believe it or not) was grits and grunts. The grits were always the same; only the fish changed. There were many kinds available; grouper, yellowtail, snapper, kingfish, jewfish, and bonefish…to name a few. Instead of filleting, the whole fish was used so the bones could be sucked clean, including the eyeballs that were considered a delicacy by some.

Avocado, a tropical fruit used like a vegetable, was the main choice to accompany the fish dishes. Old sour, made from key limes was used to garnish the fish. Fried plantains were another popular choice for almost any kind of meal.

Turtle was also another mainstay in the Key Wester's diet. It was made into steaks at times, but mostly steamed or stewed, along with vegetables and lots of gravy…served over rice to make it go a long way.

Other seafood, readily available, were stone crab, conch, and crawfish that were used in many combinations to create incredible dishes that eventually made names for themselves.

Grits, potatoes, rice, yellow cornmeal, and lots of gravies were the magic foods that made the difference between feast or famine.

Not to be outdone, the homemade soups were always a welcomed change - to the nostrils as well as to the stomach. The most popular were black bean, lima bean, vegetable beef soup and beans and corn soup. Pigeon peas were usually made into hoppin' johns, a combination of rice and peas, cooked one-one, where every grain of rice tasted like a pigeon pea.

The most exotic of the soups was souse, a conglomeration of pigs' feet and chitterlings, tripe and other pig parts. It was served as the main dish at times, along with hot buttered Cuban bread. However, many preferred to serve it along with grits and avocado as side dishes. It was always garnished with old sour and many used red hot bird peppers. It was a rarity to be treated to the dish because it involved too much work and was so costly.

A special dessert along with hot, homemade sweet potato bread was as much a part of bean soup day as the beans. Equally as important, were the jokes that were insinuated and the laughter that ensued which had a way of turning the plain meal into a festive occasion.

Selecting the best dessert from the array that could be produced from the kitchen at 719 Francis Street is an impossible task. However, circumstances of the day determined the dessert of the day.

It was a matter of routine to whip up a key lime pie, sometimes made with a crust of crushed graham crackers with whole crackers encircling the pan.

Guava duff, the kind you boil in a can, served with egg sauce, had to be timed for the season when the fruit was ripe. Three-tier coconut layer cake and chocolate layer cake were mouth-watering experiences. Not to be over-looked, was the queen of all pudding, made with boxed guava jelly (with the eye)…a crowning glory…fit for a queen. Syrup cake (my favorite) made with raisins, dates and nuts, according to taste, was more than you could bear. Varied pies, custards, puddings, and many other varieties were considered the easy in-betweens.

Speaking of sweets, candy making was an exciting past time for our family. It didn't have to be for a special celebration; they took time and made it special. In not long, the kitchen became like a beehive with the buzzing in preparation for the sweet event. Everyone put their two cents in. Their specialties were caramels (fudge), divinity fudge, fresh coconut candy in various colors and pull candy in many flavors - the most fun to watch. All the tugging, pulling and folding took two to stretch and pull the candy over and over, then fold and repeat the process for what seemed like a long time. Everyone took turns.

The laughter and chatter were as much a part of the candy-making process as the ingredients. In competition to these carryings on, the children's fight over who would get the remains off the stirring spoon or who would get to scrape the pot for any leavings, all added to a scrapping good time. Sharing the delights had to be dealt with delicately - but everyone always seemed to be able to rise to the occasion without much ado.

Making the most of what you had was the key to success back then. There was such a thing as being in need at times, and at others, there was more than enough. The secret lies in making yourself content in either situation. I like to think that trickery and magic played a role too, like making something out of nothing. There was definitely an art involved in the scheme of things that withstood the test of time. There were good times and there were lean times, but, all in all, they were memorable times worth preserving forever. I look at my past like a fingerprint that dictates who I am and the island of Key West is part and parcel of that package. The place where we live plays a big role in who we are.

From my perspective, Key West is magic; that will never change for me. It has cast its spell in many lives, and will continue for years to come. However, as the island changes, so will the magic. It will take on a different form to accommodate the newcomers who seek to transform the island with their new trends. They look for much but can come to little, by manipulating the "way things were."   There is one consolation for everyone involved, the sun will still rule by day and the moon and stars will rule by night - nothing can be added and nothing taken away.

In my kind of years, the island conjures up imagery of peace and contentment; there weren't any other choices. There was always a cohesiveness of spirit among the islanders that still prevails today; the kind dreams are made of. Whenever there was any resistance to change, the reason had to be they could not find anything that could be improved upon.   They were protective of all that mattered in the world as they knew it - the famous Rock of Renown.   If the islanders had a motto, it would have to read, *our town now and forever*.

Somewhere beneath the surface you could sense the emotions that ran deeper than you could imagine. No one could deny the beauty of the island and all it offered.   It was a unique gift, with all the trimmings, wrapped in a sea of ribbons and fringed in skirted palms that appeared to dance the hula to the music of the ocean breezes; a package of tranquility and constancy, like the neighborhoods that never changed.   All the homes looked alike and the people lived alike…or so it seemed. There were no gated communities needed for protection or to divide the people from the haves or the have nots; nor were there any cars (to speak of), much less two car garages to distinguish the classes or status quo.   Your worth was measured by your kindred spirit - there was no reason to look any further than that.

There is contentment in the thought of everything staying the same, day in and day out, and in our heart of hearts, that's the way our island will always remain.

Much of the magic of the island is to be found within the people, the native Key Westers who are proud to keep their past to the forefront - there's no reason not to. For those who seek the magic of the island, first, you must strive diligently to understand its people. Through gaining insight into their past experiences, you will witness the magic in the present…it's as simple as that.

I like to think of my family in terms of a patchwork quilt that had its patchy and scrappy times in all its many twists and turns, and during its ups and downs along the vertical and through the rows of separation. Even so, they alternated smoothly along the horizontal while seeking a balance to sustain the whole framework of the family picture. Life is not always a serious proposition, as reflected in some of the colorful scraps of the past that formed patches for the future.

Some stand out in brilliant hues while others tell a different story in their more subdued shades that form the background. Regardless, all the patches are important as the others; the whole no less, no more, in relationship to one another.

Through the combination of colors in the patterns and designs, you can see how similarities and differences can establish compatibility and be brought into a relationship of harmony and unity with one another.

The quilt could not be completed without Uncle Lewis. He is of medium build and big on talent. You may have to search closely within the subdued shades to find him, because that is where he would prefer to be. However, he comes to the forefront in the brighter hues, at times, but always on his own terms.

To some, he may have appeared idle and lazy as he tinkered endlessly with an old watch, but those efforts eventually developed into a successful watch repair business. He converted Ma Pierce's old washroom in the back yard into a well-organized watch repair shop. It wasn't long he made a name for himself and people came from all over the town, bringing any and everything that refused to tick or tock.

While growing that trade, he began working on someone's old car and in time, became a top notch mechanic, in more demand than he allowed.

It was obvious from the start; he relished his independence and refused to give it up under any circumstances. His craft served him well for as long as he wanted it to. His choices definitely indicated his preferences and that never changed. His day always went according to his mood…suffice it to say.

Uncle Lewis' successes did not depend upon his disposition. He appeared abrupt...a man of few words. If a statement needed five words he would say it in three. He went straight to the point of any matter with no furbelows attached. If a person asked him, "How long do you think the job will take?" His curt reply would be, "When it's done." Another question posed, "When will you begin working on the car?" His answer might be, "Some day."

Regardless of the day or time involved, anything he did was to perfection and that was his stock in trade. Everyone learned to overlook or accept his mannerisms; they were as consistent as his skills.

In pursuing mechanics, he came across a stumbling block - he was left handed and all tools were made for right handed people. Some parts of the motor were almost impossible to deal with so he invented all the left handed wrenches and tools he needed. These were new inventions and he could have gotten patents and become a millionaire many times over, but never pursued that option. All of the family still bemoans what could have been for him.

His talents did not stop there. Eventually, he became a master carpenter but only worked for a select few periodically..."as the notion strikes," he would tell anyone. Those who wanted him for special jobs were willing to compromise and accepted his schedules.

When Uncle Lewis wasn't working, he was creating lasting and useful things, like the beautiful porch chairs he designed and built for the family's comfort and enjoyment. As time elapsed, they too, were copied and made popular as they grew in demand. During those young years, he met and married a girl who became his one and only - Rowalder. They had two children, Elsie Lee and Howard.

It was obvious; Uncle Lewis viewed his world on a half and half basis; half work and half play. No doubt, to him, playing meant creating - his lifelong hobby.

Believe it or not, he could be "down to earth" and humorous, like when he played his mouth organ for the family sing-alongs that took place on the front porch almost every night. He was self taught and could play many renditions besides the family's requests as the evening wore on. When he had to fake a song he didn't know, the family was in for a treat. He became hilarious, bending his head in rhythmic motions as his hands trembled with tremolos and his mouth slid up and down with wild glissandos while searching for the right pitches. The more we laughed, the more he faked with incredible embellishments.

Everyone knew the night was coming to a close when he made the unusual announcement, "And now for the Gillette song," Gi-Let Me Call You Sweetheart, his favorite play on words. All of us knew the song but could hardly sing for laughing. This was the case where something old always became new again.   All in all, he was very entertaining and left a lasting impression on his audience.

Above and beyond all his previous accomplishments, there were more to come. He definitely moved into a more prominent and celebrated position on the quilt when he presented the family with a new, homemade pachisi game - one of his finest masterpieces. We were shocked beyond reproach. It was our most favorite indoor activity. We had worn our small cardboard game into a frazzle. His handiwork looked like a beautiful work of art. It was a large, brightly painted, sturdy folding board that appeared indestructible, with all the markings to perfection. He cut the moving tiles out of discarded, colorful toothbrush handles, shaving and sanding them to a smooth and glossy finish. Pachisi took on even a greater appeal than before. If there is any way to earmark this unforgettable memory, it would have to be a patch that is one of a kind, engraved in stitches of gold.

The quilt takes on a more luminous quality as Uncle Lester makes his entrance at center stage in the most brazen swatch in the block that glistens like sequins and glows in the dark, regardless of the angle from which you view it. He illuminated any room he entered and never ceased to entice an audience, without any effort on his part.

He was a handsome, light brunette, built like a model. His debonair walk was enough to reveal all that was needed to understand the magnetism he had in captivating an audience, family and friends, alike, (he never knew an enemy.) He was one of a kind and his family adored him.

Uncle Lester was a strong thread woven securely within the family patterns; sometimes on the horizontal, but at other times, on the vertical. Regardless of the direction, when at the crossroads, he chose the right path to his future - putting family first - that lifelong practice never wavered.

The glitter of his love was evident in all walks of life, whether near or far; anywhere, anytime, and it appeared in many forms. That's how a close-knit family has to be in order to reap all the treasures that only a family can share with one another. Preserving unity gives peace which binds you together - united in love.

Uncle Lester created an aura of *all's right with the world*, the moment he appeared in your presence. That alone, brought a smile to your face and in not long, laughter was sure to follow - that you could count on. He could turn anything about face or inside out if necessary to reach the happiest outcome. Simply put, he was like a good dose of medicine for whatever ailed you. His personality was definitely his stock in trade.

Ever so often, on entering the home, he would throw open the door as if he was making his debut at center stage - ready to perform in his own production.

He began to compose his own script, like he had done many times before, as he stomped heavily up the hallway, nearing the kitchen, where he could usually find a receptive audience. He had a way of creating an opportunity to perform when none presented itself. Any time he determined something was a kilter, he used that as his cue to go into action, hamming it up with assertive gestures and capers to match.

By the time he had his audience in fits of laughter, he would tramp over to a small, triangular closet in the corner of the dining room. At that moment, everyone suspected what was coming next; regardless, the anticipation was as great as the actuality.

As if by magic, with one sweep of his hand...PRESTO! Smack in the middle of the dining room table, he deposited the brown, molded replica of a life-sized lump of dog dung; a feces, criss-crossed in exact proportions! Everyone laughed until they cried. Each performance was as great a hit as if it was the first...but only when he played the role.

I don't know where that family heirloom originated. My guess is Uncle Lewis probably created it. I do know, if I had it today, I would place it among my most prized possessions; not because of its looks but for its deeds. I would use it as an example to teach my generation how important it is to look for hidden riches in secret places - the ones that can't be figured in dollars and cents.

Uncle Lester was a free spirit and a daring one. When you couple a dynamic personality along with an adventuresome nature, the combination has an explosive quality that produces combustion where lots of things can happen - and they did.

Most noteworthy, at the time, was the motorcycle craze. He was about seventeen or eighteen when that came about. It wasn't long, two or three of his friends followed suit and they called themselves a gang. Revving motors that spewed fumes everywhere and the skidding of brakes, along with other motorcycle antics, enveloped the neighborhood.

Just about the time he considered himself a skilled rider, the unthinkable happened. A big carnival came to town and its main feature was the *wall of death*. This involved a tremendous, circular, barrel-like structure (about two stories high and one story in circumference) where a motorcycle would ride from ground level, in circles to the top, without going over the edge, then return to where you began - hopefully alive!

The sound alone was intolerable as the cyclist accelerated and shifted to make the climb. I can still remember the warm-up; revving and gunning the motor, and then the shift into gear as it slowly began its journey of death to the top. The higher it climbed, the louder it got as it vibrated the walls. Our hearts skipped beats every time the motor plopped and fought to gain its rhythm. The element of speed in accelerating and decelerating seemed to be crucial in maintaining the delicate balance between life and death.

All of this was scary enough, but when Uncle Lester took the dare to ride the contraption, all the family went ballistic. Ma and Pa Pierce were uncontrollable, but no amount of persuasion could make him change his mind. It was like a big joke to him and he assured everyone there was nothing to worry about - not that his words held much weight.

Most of the family stayed home when the event took place. Three or four of us stood in hearing distance to await the outcome, hoping against hope that he would change his mind the last minute. We squeezed each other and prayed while it was proceeding. A mixture of fear and dread seemed like an endless chasm. Needless to say, he rode it like a champ, safely to the top and to the ground again. He was ecstatic with his success and the instant stardom he had attained in many people's eyes, but not in his family's. I'm sure the experience lasted him a lifetime. It remained the topic of conversation in our family for many years to come and is still recanted today.

It wasn't long, life returned to normalcy as everyone got back into the old routines of everyday life. All seemed right with the world until the family realized Uncle Lester had made a disappearing act. Ma and Pa Pierce were use to him taking short stints where he would leave and return without a word in between, then suddenly appear in the front door as jolly as Old Saint Nick. But this time was different. He had been gone what seemed forever and Ma Pierce's intuition led her to know, he "was off to see the world," as he had made known he would do some day. She cried every day for her "wondering boy" and his safe return.

During this time, after such a lengthy number of months, the family had come to terms with the inevitable; Uncle Lester must be dead and buried in some unmarked grave - no telling where.

Just as hope was giving way to hopelessness, a long, slick, black limousine pulled up to the curb at 719 Francis Street. Almost immediately, all the family gathered to view, what appeared, at first glance, to be a hearse. A mixture of fright and suspicion enveloped their beings. They gawked in awe as a dignified, handsome, uniformed young man got out of the car and walked around to open the door for the elderly gentleman. The family had never witnessed such grandeur and regal formality. As the two men approached the porch together, Ma and Pa Pierce were the first to recognize their prodigal son, whose arrival had the effect of a Second Coming. It was the most overwhelming and joyous occasion beyond their wildest dreams. Pa Pierce even danced his original jig, kicking up his heels in the air while he shouted, "Frit tra la la la boomba," a select performance exhibited only on the most momentous occasions.

Amid happy tears with the glorious homecoming, the family finally learned, first hand, all about his episodes from the time he left home that fateful day. He went into detail how he became a hobo, catching trains to far off places and landing in jail at times. He described how he made it big in Cleveland Ohio, where he met a very wealthy, old man, Mr. Bainey, who learned to adore him and hired him as his private chauffeur, had him dress in formal attire to suit the job, and escort him around the world. Along the way, Uncle Lester learned to dine in elegant places and was taught the proper etiquette for the formalities. All improprieties (and there were many) was a form of entertainment for Mr. Bainey and were dealt with in laughter and gratitude; emotions shared equally by both.

As they listened intently, they couldn't help but feel Mr. Bainey not only saved their sons' life, but gave him a new life. Right from the start, Mr. Bainey and the family shared mutual respect and deep regard for one another. After this trip, he had his prodigy bring him back for a visit every year.

When Mr. Bainey died, Uncle Lester headed for Detroit, Michigan, where he was successful in making big money working in an automobile plant. As a matter of routine, he always shared some of his bounty with his family. In later years, I remember being told by my mother how he salvaged the home during the depression, by having a new roof put on.

That same year, his sister, Gina, in her senior year of high school, faced having to quit in order to work and help support the family. Besides, there was no money for the costly activities, like the prom, the graduation ring, the fancy clothes, and other incidentals. Uncle Lester rallied to the cause by insisting his sister graduate and sent all the money for her expenses and for all the family's as well. Being a Good Samaritan was only one of his attributes.

It was during this period of time, he met and married a wonderful Polish girl, Mary. They had met when he rode an elevator she was operating. In a few short years, they had an adorable baby girl they named, Sharon. Now they were three... and that's how they always remained, near and dear to each other for all the years that life allowed.

During those early years they settled in Key West where all the family still remained. They too, like all the other members of the family, continued in the tradition by beginning their new life at 719 Francis Street. Eventually, he became independently wealthy by building his own home and many rental properties, and became a jack-of-all-trades - fixing any and everything that was fixable.

Speaking of traditions, they brought one with them...a part of Mary's heritage - it was called the polka. Mary had taught the dance to Uncle Lester while they were living in Detroit. Not long, after they arrived on the island, it became a tradition in Key West after the dynamic duo was seen dancing the polka during a party celebration in one of the popular clubs in town. There was a big audience, including some family members watching the command performance. From that moment on, any time the pair was attending any event where there was music, the band would get a signal to begin a polka. If the couple hesitated, the clapping of hands and stomping of feet persisted until they took center stage.

Their performance was an extravagant display from start to finish. They would stand poised in each others arms waiting for the music to begin. As the band struck the first note, their heads began to tilt in the lead while their feet skipped in rhythmic steps and their bodies followed in swift pursuit. They would swirl from side to side, dipping and turning as they circled the entire dance floor. Occasionally, they stopped for a stomp, stomp, stomp, in unison on select beats...then began another repetition. Everyone always hated to see it come to an end.

They seemed like two peas in a pod as they smiled to each other during the exhibition - a blissful display that made them the envy of any ordinary couple. It is a picture perfect memory...one that will never be discarded and can never be replaced...my heart tells me so.

Memories are like powerful, instant replays of past experiences that we have no control over. At the time, there is no way to tell when an experience will become a memory or how valuable it will be until it withstands the tests of time. The best ones seem to originate out of nothing and proceed to become something. You can't measure meaning, nor live without memories. When a person tries to discard their past, they lose all sense of belonging. The more you limit your relationship with your family, the more distant you are from yourself.

Building memories with your family are the most important gifts to give to them and to yourself. Limiting family relationships, limits who you are or who you could ever hope to become. Don't be afraid of bad memories. The way to prevent them is to overpower them with good ones.

A family is one body. Each member is part of the body and if one part suffers, all the other parts suffer with it. Put behind you what you must and reach for all that lies ahead...together, in love.

One of my most cherished memories originated in a name. I was always Povie Eviee to my Uncle Lester and for many years, never thought to question why. In time, my mother revealed how I acquired that name and that's where the real value enters the picture in my life.

Mother disclosed, Uncle Lester was a pre-mature baby and had to battle for his life a lengthy time. Due to the unfortunate beginning, he was a late bloomer in developing skills according to his age and speech was one area where he had the most difficulty. At a tender age, he was told by my dad he had to call me by my full name - Florence Evelyn (orders to the entire family to prevent nick names.) The closest Uncle Lester could get to pronounce those monstrosities, was, Povie Eviee... so that's who I became to him and him alone, forever. It seemed like fate had created this special bond between us for the rest of our lives. Recognition has a sneaky way of igniting a nobody into a somebody.

After learning its humble beginning and the circumstances surrounding its existence, I viewed it as the most valuable gift I ever received and I still feel that same way today. It came with a lifetime guarantee and didn't cost anyone a cent. A gift of yourself is the most valuable gift you can give; one whose worth is impossible to measure.

Over the years, every time he walked in and out of my life, that gift grew in value as he called me Povie Eviee, smiled so broadly and playfully rumpled up my hair. At moments like those, it was as if I received a crown from His Royal Highness - it meant as much to me. It was a once in a lifetime gift of long ago that kept giving over the years until Uncle Lester took it with him when he went away for the last time in 1993.

Remembrances of Uncle Lester come in many forms. A flood of emotions are ignited every time I hear the wail of a freight train in the distance, hearing its iron wheels stammer on the lonesome tracks as it nears, continuing to somewhere - only hobos know the answers to the language of the rails. The clicking and clacking echoes far into the distance until it finally vanishes as it heads towards its destination...but not before it has left me misty-eyed and forlorn with thoughts and feelings that I should have reconciled long ago.

I want Povie Eviee back again - just one more time, but my heart tells me that can never be, except in memories where I will keep it preserved for as long as I'm allowed.

I experienced the same emotions when Kirk allowed me to join in a game of marbles with the boys, where I received special recognition. At those times, Kirk became "Kirkie" to me. The only distinction between the two experiences were, instead of receiving a crown, I received the glory. The effects were the same.

The more powerful a memory is the more we want to relive that experience, again, and again; but I have to remind myself, the past is beyond my reach, embedded in memories.

A family is like a stairway to heaven and our heritage - the roadmap to that future. Take my hand and let me lead you; walk with me up the path in the imagination of our hearts where all the secrets lie. That walk must be controlled by love because that is where you find all the treasures of life. Write your own script along the way so you can star in your own production in the theater of life. We all have a role to play and our performance depends upon one another as we bring with us all we have received by tradition.

Uncle Lester was only one rung in the ascent to the goal. All family members played a role throughout the process. Each member of the family is part of the body - and the quilt is that body; a family who stayed and prayed together through thick and through thin.

This quilt is my family. You can recognize them in the center block where the heart is - the well-spring of life. All the intrinsic values of the family's life are captured through the compatibility of primary colors - bold and daring patterns in red that illuminate and glow in the dark; the ingenuous designs in green that sparkle with loyalty and character; the peculiar shapes in varied hues, symbolic of many mannerisms and displays of creative humor that make light of the dark. All stand out to be counted and identified, one to the other. What you can't see, you can sense through the impact of energy from the intensity of colors and symbols that concoct images of the past that come to life in green and purple within the colorful portrait. The family heirloom is as detailed as a Coat of Arms, ready to be displayed in a place of distinction.

From within the center block, beams of light reach out in all directions towards the patches and scraps of hand-me-downs that meant different things, at different times, to different people - all an integral part of the spontaneous background; recognizable remnants of long ago that produce a feeling of nostalgia that causes a rejoicing of the heart.

A transition takes place in the repetitions in different variations of the motif, creating intrigue and furnishing insight into the different personalities, so we can discern between the matters of the heart and the acceptable sacrifices.

Just as important, are the whimsical flip flops seen in unexpected places, creating humorous oddities in their role of reversals, making the old seem new again as their staccato rhythms entertain us and enhance their surroundings.

In sharp contrast, three heart-shaped appliqués of special recognition, hand-sewn with gold and silver ballion thread features three names in positions of renown; Ma and Pa Kemp; Ma and Pa Pierce; and my Mother and Father - all exquisitely decorated in gold on a background of silver - bordering the center block as prominent as they are permanent. The glittering array of gold and silver only partially gives justice to all they represent and mean to me.

Gold and silver threads embellish the passages as they weave throughout the masterpiece, creating a common bond, like DNA, authenticating the traits and characteristics of the family.

Variations on the theme appear in the tell-tale signs of His Great Lights, where piecing creates a moving feeling, in shades and shadows of gold. They play in syncopated rhythms with the cloudy caricatures, under the heavenly canopy that hovers over the variegated garden deeply rooted below in memory lane.

Just a short distance away from that rendition, where the sea meets the shoreline, we modulate into another major key that transposes the seascape into a border that binds and frames the living quilt like a wreath, in harmony with all its moving parts - secured upon a sound foundation.

Not to be overlooked in the orchestration, are the coconut palms; the sea gulls, sprinkled like salt and pepper on the nearby bank; sailboats bobbing like man-o-wars and even the lighthouse is visible in the distance. It is not an illusion. For those who can't see the entire scene doesn't mean it's not there.

The quilt is music - played by the greatest instruments on earth. Its repertoire was built around a family's life on an island throughout all the arrangements; from peaceful interludes to movements in the strictest counterpoint.

It is evident at a glance, a quilt like this is not an ordinary quilt, and in the finale, you will have to agree, it is one that will persevere, to be handed down from generation to generation. The quilt is my song - A Melody of Love. It is my everything.

Our family is forever. There is no Returns Department, so if there is anything you can't accept, you must forget. You may find the answer you're looking for in the treasure hunt, where love is, or in the Lost and Found Department - deep within yourself. Love is found in many obvious and obscure places; you just have to discover it. Sometimes, all we have to give, is ourselves. Our family is our all in all.

Anyone who abandons their family becomes a person they're not supposed to be. They're like an impostor - out of touch with themselves.

When all is said and done, memories are all we're left with. They're not just for old time's sake. They are our yesterdays, and as life unfolds, they become our tomorrows. Secure your memories in your heart, the safety deposit box of the soul, along with all your other aspirations...for the longer you keep them, the more valuable they become. There is no end to the story as long as our tomorrows last.

During my life, I have been given great gifts and precious moments, but the greatest of these is my family - where my life began and where I want it to end.

In the beginning, was the neighborhood, where life's recollections begin. Our neighborhood was our world. There are some that are unique within their own right. There are many that appear to be from the same mold, identical in most respects. Some we want to remember - others we'd like to forget. But a childhood neighborhood is different. It symbolizes life that is as much a part of our being as breath itself, whether we know it or not. It is immortal; a part of us that can not be erased or relived - except in memories, and never replaced - but then - who would want to?

Lighthouse

Tomb

About the Author

Named, Florence Evelyn Drudge, when she was born in 1927 at 719 Francis Street in Key West, Florida, where she lived most of her early childhood - living in Key West, most of her life.

She was educated in the Key West schools, with the exceptions of brief intervals when she attended Miami schools and a one-room schoolhouse (where all twelve grades were taught) in Tavernier, Florida.

She began her career in music at an early age, studying private piano over the years. During this same time, she took tap dance classes regularly. As fate would have it, years down the road would find her studying tap at a famous studio in Detroit, Michigan, where Shirley Temple had previously studied. At this period in her life, her dancing capabilities were as pleasing to her as her music studies. She recalls, in Tavernier, Florida, gaining a brief celebrity status when she was awarded first prize in a big competition talent show (for all ages) held in the theater (now a hotel), when she sang, then tapped to a song, *Mammy, Mammy*.

When she was graduating from Key West High School in 1945 (where she excelled in varsity sports), she was graduating from music, under the direction of Sister Mary Elizabeth at the convent of Mary Immaculate in Key West. At this same time she was performing her graduate work, she was receiving her music teacher's certificate from the Sherwood Music School of Chicago - made possible through correspondence courses under the leadership of Sister Mary Elizabeth.

Throughout this period, she had already begun her serious career in teaching. At seventeen years old, her future life's ambitions had begun to be realized. All she felt was needed, was more background.

Eventually, she married and while raising her four children, she took advanced organ instruction at the

University of Miami, while continuing to teach full schedules of piano lessons within her home.

In the meantime, she was given the great honor and privilege to return to the convent to teach piano along with Sister Mary Elizabeth and Sister Margaret in the expanding music department. She considered this experience an exceptional education within itself. The music hall was *art in action* from every direction - at all times. From the many practice cubicles in melodic pursuits, to the incredible ever changing decorations that educated and entertained in every corner of the hall, the decorum, and the exacting professionalism in recitals - there is not enough space to give justice to all the music hall embodied.

The Sisters had a way of bringing out the very best within each individual, where each child could become a prodigy within their own right.

In 1972, she graduated with honors, with an Associate in Arts degree, at the Florida Keys Community College.

In 1986-1987, she began to further her education at the University of Florida, in Gainesville (while playing tennis at the university with a local team - the Lady Gators.) She arrived at the senior level when she had to put her ambitions on hold due to putting family first.

After sixteen years, she began her first professional attempt to write a book that one of her professors had previously advised her to do.

This book is her first attempt at combining the visual arts with the musical arts - hoping the key that unlocked one door will open another for her.

IN MEMORY

This labor of love is in memory of my first child, a son, Charles Brent White; born July 27, 1948, in Key West, Florida - June 3, 2001.

I am thankful for all the time we had together, and no one can ever fill that special spot in my heart that I keep reserved for him, alone.

I feel assured, the love and support we gave to each other over the years, exemplifies all that a parent-child relationship was ordained to be.

Brent was the energizer of my soul and spirit during the many hours it took to complete my book. Without him, I would have been at sea without a compass. Though he is absent in the flesh, he is with me, forever, in the spirit.

ISBN 141201837-4